'AFTER THIS MANNER PRAY YE'

'After this Manner Pray Ye'

STUDIES IN THE LORD'S PRAYER

BY

A. H. MᶜNEILE, D.D., C.F.,

Fellow of Sidney Sussex College, Cambridge.
Author of "Self-Training in Prayer."

WIPF & STOCK · Eugene, Oregon

Wipf and Stock Publishers
199 W 8th Ave, Suite 3
Eugene, OR 97401

After this Manner Pay Ye
Studies in the Lord's Prayer
By McNeile, A. H.
Softcover ISBN-13: 978-1-6667-6103-0
Hardcover ISBN-13: 978-1-6667-6104-7
eBook ISBN-13: 978-1-6667-6105-4
Publication date 10/4/2022
Previously published by W. Heffer & Sons, 1919

This edition is a scanned facsimile of the original
edition published in 1919.

CONTENTS.

CHAP.		PAGE
	PREFACE	vii
	INTRODUCTION	viii
I.	OUR FATHER	1
II.	OUR FATHER	10
III.	THY NAME, THY KINGDOM, THY WILL	20
IV.	OUR DAILY BREAD	32
V.	FORGIVENESS	43
VI.	TEMPTATION AND EVIL	54
VII.	THE KINGDOM	62
VIII.	THE POWER	72
IX.	THE GLORY	82

*O*UR Father, which art in heaven, Hallowed be thy Name : Thy kingdom come : Thy will be done : in earth as it is in heaven. Give us this day our daily bread. And forgive us our trespasses, as we forgive them that trespass against us. And lead us not into temptation ; but deliver us from evil.

For Thine is the kingdom, the power, and the glory, for ever and ever. Amen.

PREFACE.

THE addresses recently given at a Retreat are here reproduced at the wish of some of those who heard them. Whatever else the war is doing it is causing most people to think, and a good many to pray. The suggestions in these pages, therefore, are offered on the chance that some of them may prove helpful in this direction.

A. H. McNeile.

Cambridge, October, 1916.

INTRODUCTION.

IN *Self-Training in Prayer* an attempt was made to arrive at an understanding of what prayer really is, and also to define its methods—prayer of utterance, of thought, and of union, or petition, meditation, and contemplation.

The first of these is the simplest. And since our Lord in His teaching on earth dealt with simple souls—' unlearned and ignorant men '—He gave them a specimen to shew the lines along which the method of petition would be most effectual. According to S. Matthew's account He prefaced it with the words 'After this manner (literally Thus) pray ye.' This shows that the Lord's Prayer is not a magic; the mere repetition of it is not effectual, but the spirit which breathes in it. We need have no hesitation in believing that nineteen centuries of thought and inspiration have taught us to find more meaning in the Prayer than was possible for the disciples when they first heard it. They must themselves have been led to find more meaning in it as the supreme events of the subsequent months taught them gradually the true Nature of Him who had given it to them, and therefore of the God whom He revealed. No one can hope to compose a series of sentences which more perfectly expresses the true spirit of petition ; but all that we find in it we must express not only in the actual wording of the Prayer but also in the wording of all our petitions.

But while we use it to standardise our own petitions, we can use it also directly in two ways.

1. We may make it a frequent subject of meditation, taking it clause by clause, spending on each as much time as we like, and as we find fresh depths of meaning in them translating them into prayers of our own. Thus the second of the three methods of prayer will supply us with fresh material for the first.

2. The first person pronouns employed throughout are ' our,' ' us,' ' we,' not ' my,' ' me,' ' I.' The Prayer is therefore to be used for others beside myself. And we can add endless varieties of meaning to it if we make it a habit to apply the words with the intention of interceding for this, and that, particular person or object. Since mankind is one, we can always unite ourselves with those for whom we pray. And the Prayer will thus become the centre from which radiate all our prayers for others, and the burning focus of all our intercessions.

I. OUR FATHER.

A FRENCH philosopher once said, 'If the triangles were to make a god for themselves they would give him three sides.' And he meant, quite rightly, that no one can speak or think of God except in terms derived from his own nature and experience. What, then, does 'Our Father' mean to a Christian? We must first go back behind Christianity. A savage chief thinks of God as the greatest of all chiefs. And the Israelites, in their primitive days, were not much in advance of that. They were a fighting tribe which emerged from the desert and seized Palestine. And they were sure that their God had seized it for them. God was the greatest of all tribal chiefs, their Judge, Ruler, Commander. But the usual title of a tribal chief was 'Father.' The name Abram, for instance, means 'High Father,' or 'Exalted Chief.' It was not till shortly before our Lord's time that a few of the more spiritual minds in Israel began to think of God as their Father in a more intimate, personal sense. But then came Jesus Christ, who talked as no one had ever talked before. He did not dwell on national privileges; He did not speak, in the popular manner, of God as the national God. But He made the Fatherhood of God the first and chiefest thought in human life. God was the close, intimate, personal Father of every man, woman, and child. We have heard His teaching so often that it is difficult for us to realise that the emphasis which He laid on the divine Fatherhood was a new departure in human thought. A small child in the slums, or away in some remote country village, perhaps thinks of the King of England as a great, mysterious person, possessed of fabulous wealth and power, an almost supernatural being in gold and purple, with a crown on his head, and everyone bowing down to him. That was very much what the Jewish man in the street thought about God when Jesus Christ was on earth. And then he was told that this transcendent Being was his very own Father, who loved him, and cared intensely about every minute detail of his daily life.

But the natural question arose: What is God really like? If the King of kings and Lord of lords is also my Father, I want to see Him—not think of Him far off, but see Him close, as a

Father ought to be. ' Lord, shew us the Father. And the answer was, ' He that hath seen Me hath seen the Father.' Our Lord often spoke of ' your Father,' and often of ' My Father ' ; but He never coupled Himself with the disciples, as though God were Father in the same sense to them and to Him. Right through the Gospels He makes His claim to be the Son of the Father. And the disciples who lived with Him day and night for some months gained the conviction that the claim was not the supreme delusion but the supreme truth of the world's history. In seeing His holiness, purity, strength, and love, they knew exactly what the character of the Father was.

And then another truth took possession of them. It was impossible for the Man Jesus to live throughout those months with a chosen group of intimate friends without His character flowing into them. But that meant the character of the Father. So that what they saw and handled concerning the Word of Life gave them fellowship, real union of spirit, with the Father and the Son.

But it was not enough for the world that eleven men should receive this fellowship. As long as the Man Jesus walked the streets and fields of Palestine, subject to the limitations of an ordinary human bodily life, He could not come into personal contact with the whole world of men. But when He was glorified through death and resurrection, the divine Influence poured out from Him was available for all men for ever. It came upon the earliest group of disciples with a sudden sweep of ecstasy, like flames of fire and a rushing mighty wind. Something came from the Son of God, that is from God Himself, and flowed into them. When one person influences another, it is his personality, his spirit, his very self, that flows into him. And when God influences man, it is Very God proceeding from Very God who flows into him. God's Spirit is not a thing, separate from God; it is God. And the disciples knew it by an experience which nothing could ever shake.

They learnt also a further truth. Those who had seen Jesus had seen the Father; and yet they knew perfectly well that He was not *identical* with the Person of the Father. And when the Holy Spirit flowed into them, it was the Spirit of Jesus Christ their risen Lord, and therefore also the Spirit of the Father; and yet they knew perfectly well that He was not *identical* with the Person either of Jesus Christ or of the Father.

Thus the experience—the unforgettable, unimaginable experience—of a few short months taught them in essence the truth of the Three Persons in the Unity of the Godhead.

And that is the only way in which anyone can learn it. The multitude of creeds which afterwards appeared in the Church, and which grew more complex and more metaphysical as time went on, consisted of so many attempts to guard the truth, to explain it in what was then modern language, to ward off this mistake and that and the other, in order to maintain in its fullness and mystery the limitless fact learnt originally by sheer experience.

This suggests a warning for all of us who work for others, or try to influence them. If we expect children, or grown up people, to start their Christianity by understanding the creeds, it is like expecting them to gain their first love of music by understanding the rules of harmony. They must, of course, be taught the rules if they are to be musicians; but when they know them by heart the rules will still leave them quite cold unless they are continually verifying their value by getting into their inmost being the spirit of harmony. When they have begun to feel, however dimly, the haunting pathos, the sensuous thrill, the elemental passions, the rippling delight, the golden glory, of music, then the rules of music will begin to take their true place ; they will help to define what the beginner is gradually learning by experience.

So that for them and for us the first question is not Do I understand the Creeds ? Am I orthodox ? Can I correctly explain the Christian doctrine of God the Three in One ? We must rather ask What has been my actual personal experience of God ?

1. Is He—is He really—to me my Father, whom I love and reverence so deeply that I shrink from grieving Him ? And is He, in my own experience, a Father who includes all that is most wonderful in a mother ? Do I know this so certainly that I am ready to trust Him absolutely ? Trust Him when things seem to go wrong, when He shows His love by sending me trouble, sorrow, need, sickness, or any other adversity ; trust Him when I feel lonely or depressed ; trust Him when I seem to be a failure ; trust Him when I am ready to cry ' My God, my God, why hast Thou forsaken me ? ' It is only when we have learnt it in life that we can make real use of the words, ' I *believe in* God the Father Almighty.' Not till then can we, with fullest meaning, pray ' Our Father.'

2. Again : is 'God the Son' merely a term employed in theology, doubtless correct, but as remote as the furthest star from any practical contact with our life ? It makes the heart bleed to think of the many so-called Christians of whom that is true. We need Him as Man, to be our nearest, closest Friend ; a Man to talk to, who understands because His sympathy is divine ; a Man who will listen to all the deepest whisperings of our souls—all the things of every day that we simply must tell to someone. Our little successes, and our big failings ; our little worriting bothers and irritations, and our big pains and sorrows and disappointments ; our little pleasures and enjoyments, and our big thrills of deep gladness. A Man who never tires of hearing us, to whom nothing is trivial, and who is never out of touch with anything human. And we need Him as God, a divine Saviour from sin ; One who is grieved with the little sins as well as with the big ones ; One on whom the Lord hath laid the iniquity of us all, and whose human heart was broken by the weight of them ; and yet God, who forgives, and cleanses, and heals. And all the creeds in Christendom won't give Him to us. We must know Him, with a growing experience, as One who is closer than a brother. Only then can we put an ever deepening

meaning into our creed : ' I *believe in* Jesus Christ, God's only Son our Lord.' Only then can we approach the fulness of meaning with which a Christian can say ' Our Father.'

3. Once more : ' God the Holy Spirit ' is to many people an abstraction—even more of an abstraction than the Father and the Son, a Name with almost no meaning at all. So we ask ourselves yet again, What has been my actual living experience of God the Holy Spirit ? We must remember, both for ourselves and others, that the experience is not the same for everyone. Some people—a few fortunate people— have received an outpouring which seemed to come almost with a sound as of a rushing mighty wind, with hot tongues of fire. God has swept upon them suddenly, and filled them with a radiant joy. They have lived through an experience—perhaps the experience of only a single minute—which nothing can ever efface. But it is not given to all Christians to know the thrill of Pentecost. The wind bloweth where, and how, it listeth. Some have felt only the faint stirrings of a summer breeze. But it is no less real, and it brings a peace and refreshment that the world cannot give. It disperses with quiet, divine power the heated, suffocating atmosphere of sin. Some people, again—a few

fortunate people—are like children who have grown up from infancy in the fresh air. They seem always to have lived, and walked, in the Spirit. They know all that they need to know about it, because they have always breathed it. But for most of us it is a struggle. The daily duties and temptations seem to keep us cooped up, as it were, in a stuffy room ; and we have to make perpetual efforts to open the window and let in the breeze. The windows seem to be so made that they cannot possibly remain open. They are not really made so ; it is our own weakness and spiritual laziness that keep them shut. Every time we manage to open them we get, by God's mercy, a living experience of the Holy Spirit. And nothing else will enable us to put real meaning into the words of our creed : ' I *believe in* the Holy Ghost, the Lord, and Giver of life, who proceedeth from the Father and the Son.'

An immediate, personal, growing experience of the Father, the Son, and the Holy Spirit, can alone make the Christian utter with the full depth of reality of which they are capable, the words ' Our Father.'

II. OUR FATHER.

'OUR Father' is the God whom we have learnt by living experience to be Father, Son, and Holy Spirit, three Persons in one God. But even that tremendous truth does not exhaust the meaning of the words. They express not only an experience, a joy, a privilege, but also a vast responsibility. Every privilege involves responsibilities ; and this is the greatest of them. Anything that we can say about God in relation to us involves a corresponding relation of us to Him. If we call Him ' Our Father ' we announce ourselves His children. And this leads to two different lines of thought. We are His children, first of all, simply because we are human beings ; ' we are His, and He made us.' And then we are His children because we are Christians.

Many of us have great need to be reminded of the first of these. The advance in every department of human knowledge feels so great that a proud independence is spreading over the human race. We feel as though we were becoming masters of the world. We know so much ;

scientific investigation can produce so much; scientific calculations can predict so much. Man in his exalted self-consciousness appears to himself to be developing into a super-man. The laws of God are becoming antiquated; right and wrong are rapidly ceasing to be distinct; and God himself is becoming an old-fashioned fancy which up-to-date people have grown out of.

Those who say ' Our Father ' give the lie to all this. And yet they don't always accept the full consequences of the words. If He is the Father Almighty, it is because He is the Maker of heaven and earth, the Fashioner and the Sovereign of all things visible and invisible. But the tendency of to-day, the intellectual atmosphere in which we move, makes even the best Christians sometimes forget His infinite Majesty and their utter, unspeakable littleness.

And some, who are not hindered by intellectual pride, are hindered by another prevalent tendency, namely to form a wrong conception of God's love, and to think of Him in a rather shallow, sentimental way as a kind, good-natured, easy-going, benevolent Being who will never be hard on us. I suppose this has come about partly from a misuse of the truth that God is always ready to forgive. ' He will not alway be chiding, neither keepeth He His anger for ever. He hath not dealt with us after our sins, nor rewarded us according to our wickednesses. . . As far as the East is from the West, so far hath He set our sins from us. Like as a father pitieth His own children, even so is the Lord merciful unto them that fear Him.' We get the general impression of such a passage, and are apt to slur the last words, ' them that *fear* Him.' It is that reverent fear that is so terribly lacking. The thought is not confined to the Old Testament. S. Paul tells slaves to serve their masters ' in singleness of heart, fearing the Lord.' S. Peter bids us ' fear God, honour the king.' Most British subjects do the latter, but for masses of people the former has very little meaning. And our Lord Himself uttered one of His most solemn warnings when He said ' I will shew you whom ye shall fear : fear Him who, after He hath killed, hath power to cast into Gehenna ; yea I say into you, fear Him.' God is our Father because He is the Infinite and Majestic Maker and Sustainer of us and of all things ; and when we pray the Lord's Prayer, or any other prayer, we ought to approach Him with a far humbler reverence and deeper awe than we usually do.

But He is our Father also because we are Christians. ' Of His own will begat He us with the word of truth.' ' As many as received Him to them gave He power to become children of God. . . who were born not of blood, nor of the will of the flesh, nor of the will of man, but from God.' And S. Paul's epistles are full of the thought of our sonship. But what does this involve ? We must remind ourselves of a truth that was grasped with special vividness in Jewish thought, and was explicitly recognised by our Lord. Think of His words in the Sermon on the Mount : ' Love your enemies, bless them that curse you, do good to them that hate you, pray for them that despitefully use you and persecute you, *that ye may be the sons* of your Father which is in heaven,' for He does the same, ' He maketh His sun to rise on the evil and on the good, and sendeth rain on the just and on the unjust. . . . Be ye therefore perfect, as your Father also which is in Heaven is perfect.' What does all this mean ? It means that children are to be a reproduction of their Father ; they are to exhibit the character of their Father ; they are to be able in a real sense, however limited, to say ' he that hath seen me hath seen the Father.'

Let us examine this wonderful truth a little more closely. We have seen that we cannot truly say ' I believe in God the Father, the Son, and the Holy Spirit,' unless we have learnt something of that truth by experience. We must learn in our own lives that God is all that a perfect Father can be ; that God the Son is all that a perfect Brother can be ; that God the Holy Spirit is all that the Spirit of a Father and a Brother can be. But the communion which we hold with the three Persons in the one Godhead must result in the possession of something which we can pour into others.

1. If God is our Father, we as His children are to reproduce Him in the world. Our influence in our work and life is to be something that can be compared with the influence of a Father— that is the true, the perfect Father, from whom, as S. Paul's says, ' all Fatherhood in heaven and earth is named.' And all motherhood is included in it. Some of the readers of these pages are parents ; some are invested with other kinds of authority or responsibility. No human being is without responsibility of some kind in relation to other lives. And you need a real, divine power that will make you, in the highest sense, helpful to everyone with whom you have to do. You need a knowledge that inspires confidence, and a strength of character that evokes respect. When S. Paul said to Titus 'Let no man despise thee,' he meant (as I have heard it well explained) ' Be the sort of person that nobody

can despise.' And you cannot get all this merely by trying to imitate the perfections of God. It is not a case of imitation. You must dwell in Him, and He in you, that His Fatherhood and Motherhood may find in you a free channel by which to pour itself out on men and women and children. The channel is obstructed, it can be entirely stopped up, by our sins, or forgetfulness of God, or lack of penitence, or spiritual inertia. It can be kept free and open only by incessant, unwearied, unvarying communion with Him.

2. The love of the Father exhibited itself in the Son. The whole series of events—His Incarnation, His perfect life of obedience, His suffering, death, and resurrection—was all one supreme act displaying the Father's self-sacrifice. ' God so loved the world that He gave His only begotten Son.' Jesus Christ so loved the world that He gave Himself. And you are to reproduce this. By union with Him you are to continue that exhibition of the Father's self-sacrifice. For more than two years self-sacrifice has been writ large across the lives of men. And yet it is possible that, from God's point of view, some of it has been partly wasted and spoiled by a mistake of man's own making. It is worth while to ask yourself whether some

of it is not undertaken merely because it is forced upon you. Is my self-sacrifice, every little detail of it, a voluntary exhibition of the love of Jesus Christ, a reproduction of the limitless love of our Father? Even though outwardly it is compulsory, it can be made voluntary if you unite yourself with Him in the doing of it. And, as before, it is not mere imitation. We are accustomed to the words 'Imitation of Christ' from the wonderful book of Thomas à Kempis; but it is difficult not to wish that another name had been given to it. It is full, from beginning to end, of the real truth, that it is a dwelling in Him and He in us. Our love, therefore, our voluntary offering and self-sacrifice, are simply His. 'I live, yet not I, but Christ liveth in me.'

And let us remind ourselves of the true meaning of Sacrifice. It does not mean simply giving up something. The word has been unfortunately vulgarised, so that we see notices of 'Enormous Sacrifices' put up in shop windows in advertisements of summer sales. But its true meaning is divine; it means something that is 'made sacred.' Every hardship, anxiety, strain or sorrow that you endure, every control of a hasty word or look or gesture when people are exasperating, every yielding up of the will and impulse, can be made a sacred thing. It can be offered to God as a continuation of Christ's passion; it can be a reproduction of His measureless sacrifice. ' I bear about in my body the dying of the Lord Jesus.' And you can do that if you keep yourself one with Him by incessant communion.

3. Once more. S. John says, ' Hereby know we that we dwell in Him and He in us, because He hath given us of His Spirit.' And His Spirit is the Paraclete. That is a word which no one English expression can translate. ' Comforter ' is part of it. If we are God's children, we are to reproduce His comforting power; and we shall do it far more by what we are than by what we say. But the comfort of the Paraclete includes every kind of moral and spiritual support, the inspiring of confidence or of hope, the uplifting of enthusiasm, the guidance of true wisdom, the healing touch of humour, the strength of encouragement, the balm of sympathy, the happiness of companionship. The shortest way in which it can be put is that ' Paraclete ' means ' One who helps.' And to that glorious office every Christian is called.

In 1 Cor. xii. 28, S. Paul enumerates some of the important offices and functions which God has appointed in His Church, and assigned to the various members, one and the self-same Spirit distributing to each man severally as He wills. We read 'God hath set some in the Church, first apostles, secondly prophets, thirdly teachers, then miracles, then gifts of healings, governments, divers kinds of tongues.' All very impressive and responsible; some readers will feel that not one of these applies to them. But in the middle of the list occurs one more, the single word *helps*. It is not the same Greek word as Paraclete, but the thought is closely similar. S. Paul uses the corresponding verb when he says ' The Spirit also *helpeth* our infirmities.' If the divine Paraclete is One who helps, you are to do His work—the work of God the Holy Spirit. And obviously this is not a case of imitation. If you do His work, it is only He is doing His work in you. S. Barnabas, for example, was the ' Son of Consolation '—' Son of *paraclesis* ' as the Greek has it—because he was ' full of the Holy Ghost.'

If, then, we pray ' Our Father,' we acknowledge a vast responsibility; as His children we accept the task of reproducing Him before men. We are to bring to bear upon everyone whom we meet the divine tenderness, care, strength, guidance, of the eternal Father; the divine love and self-sacrifice of the eternal Son; the divine comfort, encouragement, exhilaration, companionship, help, of the eternal Spirit.

But who is sufficient for these things? It makes us almost afraid to say ' Our Father ' if, whenever we say it, it involves so much. And yet, ' if our heart condemn us, God is greater than our heart, and knoweth all things.' Because we are sons and daughters of God, He ' hath sent forth the Spirit of His Son into our hearts, crying Abba, Father.' He knows all that it involves ; He can put into it the full volume of its meaning. ' Ye have received the spirit of adoption, and by that spirit we cry Abba, Father. The Spirit itself beareth witness with our spirit that we *are* the children of God,' however feeble our reproduction of Him may have been. He can say ' Our Father ' in us, and for us. We know not how to say it as we ought, ' but the Spirit itself maketh intercession for us with groanings which cannot be uttered.'

III. THY NAME, THY KINGDOM, THY WILL.

TO 'Our Father' are added the words 'which art in heaven,' and then we are bidden to pray that three things may happen 'in earth as it is in heaven.' I feel sure that that clause is intended to go with each of the three, and that 'heaven' must have the same meaning as in the opening words.

One truth which scientific research has made quite clear—and that means a truth to which the Holy Spirit has guided us—is that the earth is round and not flat. Heaven is not a place, higher up than the blue sky over our heads; it is a condition, a state, a quality. In the Aramaic language, which our Lord spoke, there is no adjective corresponding with the word 'heavenly'; but when His words about God were translated into Greek, as we have them in the New Testament, they appeared sometimes as 'My—or your—Father which is in heaven,' and sometimes as 'My—or your—heavenly Father.' The words in the Lord's Prayer, therefore, mean for us : Our heavenly Father ; Our Father whose Presence, whose Life, whose very Being, *is* heaven, the eternal Reality, and of whose activity every created thing and person is an outward and visible expression. And correspondingly we go on to pray ' Hallowed be Thy Name, Thy Kingdom come, Thy will be done, outwardly and visibly in our earthly condition as in the eternal, ideal Reality of Thy heavenly Being. This meaning of ' Heaven ' is well illustrated in the Epistle to the Ephesians. Five times (i. 3, 20, ii. 6, iii. 10, vi. 12) an expression occurs which in our English Bible is translated ' in the heavenly places.' But the word ' places ' is absent from the Greek. The apostle is speaking of the spiritual sphere, the heavenly condition of things, in which the great elemental facts of our religion are worked out. And since 'God is Spirit,' as it is said in S. John's Gospel, we can say either that God dwells *in* the spiritual sphere, *in* the all-embracing Reality that we call ' heaven,' or we can say with equal truth that God *is* ' heaven,'—' heaven ' is the Presence of God. What we want, then, to aim at is not simply ' to go to heaven when we die,' but to get something of heaven—to experience something of heaven—now ; to realise more and more fully the divine Reality now.

With this thought in our minds we can approach the second clause of the Prayer. ' Hallowed be Thy Name—in earth as it is in heaven.' God's name represents His Person and Nature. Your name puts before those who know you your being and character; it sums up in their minds all that they know about you. Let us suppose that I hear or read the name John Smith. I have never met John Smith; I have never heard anything about him. To me it is a mere name, as we say. But if I am told the smallest fact about him by somebody whom I believe to be speaking the truth, the name John Smith begins to mean something to me. Then I am told more—his occupation, his past history, something about his family, his age, his appearance. Every fresh fact enlarges for me the meaning of his name. Then I learn something of his character. Wherever I go, people always say something good about him; and his name begins to mean so much to me that I begin to wish I could get to know him. All this I can learn from the testimony of others before I ever set eyes on him. But however much I hear, however wonderful the accounts, and however fully I believe them all, I cannot say that I *know* him. I only know about him by hearsay. But at last I meet him; and what an extraordinary difference it makes! All the true accounts of him that I have received fall into their places, and begin to be *real* to me for the first time. And then I meet him often, and get to know him better and better. His name gains a continually deepening meaning for me. John Smith now represents to my mind a strength, a tenderness, a beauty, and many other things that I never dreamt of when I first heard the name.

The parable is clear. The name 'God,' the Father, the Son, and the Holy Spirit, was known to us only by hearsay when we were small children, and perhaps for long afterwards. But it meant very very little to us. But then came the wonderful change when we began to meet Him, and to know Him intimately. And the more we live in His Presence, and our intimacy and love are deepened, the more holy, sacred, wonderful, His Name becomes to us. Every time, therefore, that we say the Lord's Prayer, and really mean the words, we ask that His Name may go on becoming more and more and more hallowed to us—in earth as it is in heaven, in our human life, in our poor, weak, sinful souls, as it is in the deep, divine Reality. But since the Holy Trinity in Unity is this divine Reality, God's Name 'hallowed in heaven' involves the perfect knowledge that mutually exists between the three sacred Persons in the one Godhead; and we are really praying that our intimate knowledge of God may continually approach a little nearer to that. Hallowed be Thy Name, in us as it is in the Godhead.

But intimate knowledge of any person must have an effect on one's character for good or for evil. If John Smith is a saint, a growing knowledge of him will be a growing help to my soul. If God's Name is hallowed in us, we are gradually hallowed, sanctified, made holy in Him; 'changed into the same image from glory unto glory.'

So far we have thought of the words only as applying to those who use them. But when we say '*Our* Father,' not merely 'my Father,' we are praying for the whole world; and we ask that His Name may become hallowed by all men, that all men may meet Him and get to know Him with a deepening intimacy of friendship and reverence. It is a prayer for missions, and we ought constantly to use it as such. And, to come back to ourselves again, we have a part in the mission to the world. It may be a small part as far as our direct activities are concerned. (And by that I mean our direct activities other than prayer. By prayer we can always be missionaries to the whole world.) Our *immediate* individual work can touch only a very little world. But for all that it is our bounden duty and service to reach after holiness for the sake of others. ' For their sake I sanctify myself.' Hallowed be Thy Name in me, in order that my influence—that is Thine influence in me—may flow out ; that Thou mayest use me to bring others to know Thee, to make them meet Thee, to introduce them to Thee, and start in them that intimacy with Thee that will transfigure their lives. Hallowed be Thy Name in me, in order that it may become hallowed in others.

But this growth in intimate knowledge has another effect. All in whom God's Name is thus hallowed are drawn together in one communion and fellowship. S. Paul expresses that in a well known metaphor when he says to the Philippians ' Our citizenship is in heaven.' And he expresses the converse in writing to the Colossians and Ephesians. In his letter to the former he reminds them that before they became Christians they were alienated and enemies in their mind. In other words they were foreigners; they had no part in the citizenship which is in heaven ; God's kingdom or sovereignty, had not yet 'come' to them 'in earth as it is in heaven.' And in the Epistle to the Ephesians he comes very close to the thought that is before us. He begs them not to live like the heathen round them, who are 'alienated from the life of God because of the ignorance that is in them'; they are aliens, foreigners, not sharers in the heavenly citizenship, because they do not know God.

Here, then, is another missionary prayer, both for heathen abroad and heathen at home. May those who know Thee not, gain such a knowledge that Thy Name may be hallowed to them, and that thereby they may take their true place as citizens, and Thy kingdom come to them. And we can adopt the words of Ps. lxxxvii. 3, and find in them a divine promise. God is represented by the Psalmist as saying that one heathen nation after another will come to be citizens of Zion; and in this verse we read 'I will think upon Rahab and Babylon with them that know Me.' 'I will in time reckon Rahab —*i.e.* Egypt—and Babylon among those who are no longer foreigners alienated by their ignorance of Me.' But Egypt and Babylon had been among the most terrible of Israel's enemies in the whole course of their history. They had been slaves in Egypt, and they were carried into exile to Babylon when their beautiful city and temple were dashed to the ground and burnt. Even to those nations God's kingdom would come in earth as it is in heaven. And with the Psalmist's confident hope before us, I think we ought to use the petition constantly, and earnestly, for Germany that has lost so much of the true and intimate knowledge of our Father. And if we do, we can trust in the divine promise : ' I will think upon Germany, Austria, and Turkey, among them that know Me.'

But we must use it also for ourselves and for England. Knowledge of God is a growing thing. His kingdom, His divine sovereignty, can ' come ' to us gradually and increasingly. And since the sovereignty of the heavenly King implies a single, corporate body of citizens, the more deeply His Name is hallowed, and His Kingship gains a hold upon their hearts and lives, the more surely will they be welded together into a unity, ' in earth as it is in heaven,' that is a unity on earth reflecting the eternal Unity of the Holy Trinity in heaven, a unity in which, as children, we can be reproductions of our Father. And so our Lord can pray to His Father for His disciples and ask ' that they may be one, *as We are.*'

But when the sovereignty of God shall have come in perfection, when His Name is hallowed universally, and all men are really and truly reproductions of our Father, it is easy to see that the unity which this involves will be a unity of purpose. Every citizen—and there will be no aliens—will want the same thing, because he will want what God wants, as each of the Three Persons of the Holy Trinity wants what God wants. That is to say His will shall be done ' in earth as it is in heaven.' This is the consummated perfection for which we are taught to pray.

Isn't that very different from the way in which some people are apt to use the words ? A trouble, or pain, or sorrow of some kind is sent to them, and they say ' Thy will be done ' with a feeling that they are martyrs. God has allowed this to happen, so I suppose I must put up with it ; but it's rather hard on me ! Was that the state of mind of our perfect Lord Jesus when He said the words in Gethsemane ? It is the whole difference between putting up with what God wants, and *wanting* what God wants. And all our Christian life, the battle, the struggle, the race, the upward journey, the growth, the sanctification, is the gradual approach to that condition of soul in which we shall instinctively, naturally, and perfectly, want what God wants. Any animal lower than man wants, instinctively and naturally, what its fleshly nature prompts. But it is the glory, and the torture, of man that a higher self made in the Image of God has been given him. And self-crucifixion is the killing of the lower self in order that the higher self may be perfectly free to want what God wants. That is why pain and suffering seem to stand out in our lives as the chiefest element in the will of God for us. From the point of view of the lower self it must be so. 'This is the will of God, even your sanctification'; and since that involves the destruction of everything in us that opposes the will of God, it must involve suffering.

But what we greatly need is to fix our eyes not on the torture of it from the lower side, but on the glory of it from the higher side. 'Your sanctification' is for the glory of God, for the sake of others. It is one item in what S. Paul calls the 'mystery of His will,' 'the purpose of Him who worketh all things according to the counsel of His will.' And we are told in plain language what that is : ' This is the will of Him that sent Me, that of all which He hath given Me I should lose nothing.' He ' willeth that all men should be saved.' Which do we really want most, and think of most, and pray and work for most—our own salvation or the salvation of all men? To want what God wants is to sanctify ourselves for the sake of others; to grow into such union with the Father, the Son, and the Holy Spirit, that Their love for the world will be ours, Their longing to save all men will be ours. In this Prayer, then, that the Lord has taught us we ask that our will may become—not merely submissive to, or even similar to, but—identical with the will of the Holy Trinity in Unity, ' in earth as it is in heaven.' Haven't we travelled a long way from the spirit of the person who says ' God has allowed this trouble to come to me; it's rather hard on me, but I suppose I must put up with it ' ?

Let us glance again over our meditations up to this point, and remind ourselves afresh to what immense heights our Lord calls us and all mankind. When we use the words that He has taught us we proclaim ourselves children, friends, and citizens, of the God who is Father, Son, and Holy Spirit: children to reproduce ' our Father'; friends to know Him so intimately that His Name will become more and more sacred and wonderful to us; citizens bound together in a corporated unity under His sovereignty. And then something so high and great that no earthly metaphor can be found to express it—a oneness with the Holy Trinity in Unity so close that we want what He wants.

IV. OUR DAILY BREAD.

WE have been thinking of high things, God's Name, God's Kingdom, God's Will. But if these things are put first, we are then allowed to ask for the supply of human needs. 'Give us this day our daily bread.' In the words 'After this manner pray ye,' we are clearly taught that in all our prayers this order of thought must be observed. God first and man second.

But do we preserve that order? How often do our immediate needs come first? How often, indeed, do they usurp the whole of our prayer? Perhaps it is not so difficult to put Him first if we kneel down to say our prayers when life is fairly smooth and ordinary. But when a sudden emergency arises, an illness or accident to someone that we love, a prospect of work or honour that we long to realise, when perhaps there are other competitors for the post, an injury or injustice done to us by someone, a sudden responsibility, or a tiring rush of work and strain. Whatever it is we feel it very much indeed; and God's Name, God's Kingship,

God's Will, tend to be pushed for the moment into the background. But Christ wants it to become, by practice, an unfailing instinct of our soul to take our pressing individual need as an opportunity—a fresh opportunity that we eagerly embrace—of praying that God's glory may be advanced by means of it, whether we get the exact thing that we happen to want or not.

Take one of the instances that I have suggested. Someone whom you love falls ill ; perhaps he or she is to have an operation. It comes upon you with a sudden weight of anxiety that makes you feel that you can think of nothing else, and that nothing else matters. If you are a Christian you rush to your knees. But if you are a good Christian you won't simply besiege God with eager and repeated outpourings of your own immediate wish : O God, make Him well ! O God save his life ! O God don't let me be left without him ! You will rather say, O God I want Thy will to be done more than anything ; let it be done, let Thy Name be hallowed, let Thy Kingdom come a little closer to us, by this trial, by the way in which I take it, and everyone else concerned, and by the working out of Thy plans whatever they may be. And if that is really the basis of your prayer, then you can go on to say ' Lord, behold he whom Thou lovest is sick '; Thou knowest how I love him, and how I want him to be restored to health; give us this day the supply of this sore need *if* that will bring most glory to Thee.

That, I think, is the kind of thing that Christ would have us learn by the position in His Prayer of the words ' Give us this day our daily bread.' He sums it up Himself when He says ' Seek ye first the kingdom of God and His righteousness, and all these things shall be added unto you '; that is, of course, added unto you if it serves the purposes of the kingdom of God and His righteousness. This is the only practical solution of the problem of answers to prayer, a problem which troubles some people so much when they don't get what they ask for. The solution is to place ' Thy will be done ' *before* ' Give us this day our daily bread.' He will answer our prayer by giving us what we really want most—the working out of His divine plans.

This is so important that it is worth while to press it further. Look at two instances in our Lord's life. In Gethsemane He ' offered up prayers and supplications with strong crying and tears unto Him that was able to save Him from death. And having been heard for His godly fear, though He was a Son, yet He learned obedience by the things which He suffered. And having been made perfect, He became unto all them that obey Him the author of eternal salvation ' (Heb. v. 7-9). He was heard, and yet He died. God did not give Him exactly what He asked for, but something immeasurably greater.

The other instance is not, perhaps, so often noticed. After He had gone about for a time healing and preaching, welcomed by enthusiastic crowds among the simple countrymen in the North, there came the first murmurings of a storm, the growing opposition of the religious authorities. He knew that the gathering storm would finally strike Him down ; so He determined to make provision that others might carry on His work. From the whole number of His followers He would choose twelve, whom He could take away into privacy, and train during the time that was left to Him. It was a question of quite incalculable importance who these twelve were to be. Their number represented the twelve tribes of Israel. Their work was to be far-reaching and complete. They must be such men as could be endued, as He was, with power from on high, to prepare men for the kingdom of heaven. And when it came they must be fitted to bear spiritual rule in it, to remit and to retain, to bind and to loose. Never was there a selection of men on which so enormous issues hung. And S. Luke tells us that ' He went out into the mountain to pray ; and He continued all night in prayer to God. And when it was day He called His disciples, and He chose from them twelve.' The whole night was needed to ask for guidance in the choice. We can picture Him kneeling in the great, dark solitude, weighing the characters and capabilities of all His best followers. We can imagine Him saying ' Abba, Father, I know that Thou hearest me always ; Thou knowest that I want what Thou dost want ; I want Thy Name to be hallowed, Thy Kingdom to come, Thy Will to be done, in earth as it is in heaven. And for this purpose, Holy Father, give Me this day Thy wisdom ; guide Me with Thy counsel, and after that receive Me with glory. Of them whom Thou wilt give Me grant that I may lose none.' And then—a few months later, ' Have not I chosen you twelve, and one of you is a devil ' ! ' Of those whom Thou gavest Me I have lost none *except* the son of perdition,' Judas Iscariot who also betrayed Him, took money, kissed Him, and in a frenzy of despair committed suicide. Looked at on the surface it might seem to be a terrible instance of a prayer that failed. But we know that it was not so. He laid before His Father an immediate personal need, but it was on the basis of a desire that His will might be done, that His plans might be worked out for the saving of the world. And His prayer was answered, because He was led to choose, among the twelve, the man who would bring about the death which would be for the saving of the world. *The prayer that failed has never existed*, because God makes use of every real prayer in order to give, not always what we ask but, what He wants us to have. And if we are following Christ truly, we want what God wants.

But the problem of answers to prayer has another side. Our Lord says, ' Be not anxious saying What shall we eat, or what shall we drink, or wherewithal shall we be clothed ? . . . For your Father knoweth that ye have need of all these things.' ' Your Father knoweth what things ye have need of before ye ask Him.' But if so, why ask ? The problem may seem difficult to solve in theory ; but it is not so difficult in practice. When a small child wants his mother to give him something, she may know perfectly well what he wants, yet she is not quite satisfied till he asks, and says ' please.' And she will often show her love best by not giving it till he does so. And our object in praying for personal needs is not to give information as to our wants to a God who knows all things, and it is not to persuade and coax Him into giving us things that He doesn't want to give us, but to express to Him our attitude of children to a Father.

Up to this point we have thought about petitions for personal needs in general, but not for daily bread in particular. Under ordinary circumstances most of us, no doubt, get our daily bread without difficulty, and treat it as a matter of course. If we use the words of actual bread, and mean what we say, we must apply them to all poverty-stricken and hungry people. But do we mean what we say? I wonder how many hundreds of times every reader of this chapter, when he has said 'Give us this day our daily bread,' has meant literally nothing! And we should be the first to condemn the heathen with his praying-wheel. But the praying-wheel is not more ineffective than some of the prayers that we say so often with our thoughts wandering. In fact the praying-wheel is really better, because there is no pretence about it. The ignorant heathen is doing what he professes to do; he is turning a wheel.

But we profess to be *praying*. Is there anything that Christians throughout the whole Church of Christ need more than to be able to pray with reality ?

But the war is helping us. On the one hand it has led millions to experience the touch of Reality ; it has begun to make people aware of the truth expressed in the book of Ecclesiastes (iii. 11, R.V. marg.) that ' God has set eternity in their heart ' ; many have begun to feel the brooding presence of Something ; they have a perception, a sensation of God's nearness, although they do not know that it is God. And on the other hand it is forcing upon men's notice the daily needs of countless other men.

In this latter connexion a difficulty may suggest itself. ' Give *us our* daily bread ' refers to all mankind. If so, it refers to the Germans, no less than to our own men who are prisoners of war, and, in many cases, miserably underfed. How can we with any sincerity pray that the Germans may have food when we have established a blockade to prevent them getting any ? The problem can be put in such a way as to make it sound difficult. But the difficulty is not really very great. Our hearts can with perfect honesty go out in deep sympathy to the hungry, and we can pray for their bodily needs no less than for our own, *if* we do it in the way that Christ has taught us, *i.e.* if we base the petition on the larger and wider desire : ' Hallowed be Thy Name, Thy kingdom come, Thy will be done.' We can ask that the war may end, and that by its cessation all hungry people may get food ; but the large, wide basis of that is that **the war** may end in such a way as to bring glory to God. Our Father—the Germans' Father and ours—make the war to cease, and the hungry to be fed, if, and when, and by methods through which, it will help in the working out of Thy divine plans that all men may be saved, and come to the knowledge of the truth. Taken, therefore, in its right order, and used with the right motive, the petition ' Give us this day our daily bread ' can be another way of saying ' May the personal needs of every man, woman, and child in the world be supplied by Thee in such a way as to advance Thy glory.'

But that leads to another thought. Personal needs include personal spiritual needs. ' Give us this day our spiritual food.' And our Lord tells us what that was to Him : ' My food is to do the will of Him that sent Me.' The daily bread is inextricably linked with ' Thy will be done.' **Man shall not live by bread alone, but** by every word—that is by obedience to every word—that proceedeth out of the mouth of God. Could He have expressed more perfectly the condition of mind which wants what God wants? To do what God wants is food—strength, support, life, growth, satisfaction. Oh how far we fall short of it! How often obedience to God's will seems to be not food but the most horribly nasty medicine. If we don't actually refuse it, we force ourselves with a wry face to take it because it is for our good. But we ought not to want what God wants because it is for our good, but because it is an opportunity of giving Him something—giving Him love, giving Him satisfaction by working out His plans. It is more blessed to give something to God than to receive anything from Him. But in fact, that blessedness, the joy of giving, the exhilaration of self-sacrifice, the abiding peace of utter obedience, will prove to be to ourselves, in proportion as we reach it, a growing satisfaction, a spiritual food. 'Blessed is he that shall eat bread in the kingdom of God.'

And lastly, our minds turn to 'the means whereby we receive the same, and the pledge to assure us thereof.' Our prayer cannot be complete in thought until we make it mean 'Give us the spiritual food of the most precious Body and Blood of Thy Son our Saviour Jesus Christ.' That was the meaning which S. Jerome and others of the early fathers found in it. In meditating on the use which can be made of the Lord's Prayer by the Christian Church, it is impossible to leave it out.

We can use the petition for ourselves in two ways. 1. When we partake of the Holy Communion, we can pray that we may verily and indeed receive what we want to receive ; that the Body and the Blood of Christ may be to us all that we want them to be, and more. 2. When we are unable to partake sacramentally, we can use the words in making an act of spiritual communion, which we ought to do *daily*. And we can use the petition for others. ' Give *us our* spiritual bread ' is a prayer for all mankind ; and we ought constantly to make it a petition that the holy Sacrament may increasingly play the part that it ought to play in the life of all Christians. To ask for that, repeatedly and earnestly, is one of the best ways of praying that our Father's Name may be hallowed, His Kingdom may come, and His Will may be done, in earth as it is in heaven.

V. FORGIVENESS.

'FORGIVE us our trespasses, as we forgive them that trespass against us.' Let us think what we mean exactly by 'forgiveness.' It is not quite so simple a matter as some people seem to think it. One thing that we must get perfectly clear at the outset is that when God forgives us our sins it does not mean that He lets us off all punishment. Remember the words of Ps. xcix. 8 : ' Thou forgavest them O God, *and punishedst* their own inventions.' ' Whom the Lord loveth He chasteneth, and scourgeth every son whom He receiveth.' He scourgeth every child whom He hath received back to Himself by forgiveness. ' If ye be without chastisement, whereof all are partakers, then are ye bastards and not sons.' It is because we can say to Him ' Our Father ' that we expect Him to punish us in His love. And His punishment is the effects produced by sin. It may have physical effects upon ourselves ; it may do physical injury to others by heredity or otherwise. But it always has its effects upon our soul, and therefore on the souls of others. Our character is deteriorated, our will is weakened, in our upward journey we have lost ground which has to be made good. Punishment always follows sin ; we are never let off.

Forgiveness is something quite different. If God is ' our Father,' we as His children are to reproduce Him. Everyone who knows us is to know something of what the Father is like. To say ' Our Father ' is to claim the immeasurable responsibility of representing Him. But the moment we sin, we misrepresent Him. Think of an ambassador representing England at a foreign court. If he makes a mistake, if he takes some step in diplomacy which England repudiates, he is recalled from his office, and ceases to be her representative. His misrepresentation, by the very nature of the case, is a direct contradiction of his ambassadorship. That is our position with every sin. We have misrepresented the Father, whom it is our sole and only function to reproduce before men. We have forfeited the privilege of being His children ; and we could never get it back unless the Father, of His free kindness, gave it back. But if we confess our sin in penitence, He mercifully reinstates us, because His Son, who represents mankind, also perfectly represents Him. He allows us to be again in oneness with Him, so that we can represent Him once more. Remember, of course, that He scourgeth every son and daughter whom He thus receiveth. The effects of our mistake may go on indefinitely; we have wrought our own punishment. But the Father has forgiven. He has renewed the unity which has been shattered. That is why forgiveness brings peace, even though we may be suffering for years afterwards the punishment of our sin. The Greek word for ' peace ' is derived from a word which means to ' unite.' Forgiveness brings peace ; and every time we disturb it our heart is restless until He stretches out His arms, and we fling ourselves into them by penitence.

But while we represent God because we are His children, we also represent mankind because we are human. Jesus Christ lifted the truth of the oneness of all mankind to the highest plane by teaching the Fatherhood of God. The Western mind finds it hard to grasp that this oneness of all human beings is not a metaphor but a literal fact. The modern spirit of individualism tends to disregard one of the most fundamental truths in the universe. This truth is closely connected with the subject before us. How is it that any human being can dare to say to another, ' I forgive you ' ? What are we that we can adopt an attitude so lordly ? as though we said ' I will overlook the wrong that you have done me, and am graciously pleased to receive you back into my friendship.' If it were not for this principle of representation that we are studying, forgiveness of one individual by another would be the extremity of futile arrogance. It is because humanity is literally one, that human forgiveness is a profound necessity. In wronging me, the personal injury that you have done is nothing — less than nothing ; but what does matter is that in wronging me you have wronged the whole of humanity. If one member of a body is wronged, all the members are wronged with it. And if you are sorry for this, I and no one else must of necessity be the person to receive you back into union with humanity once more. When our Lord on earth, in His human life of self-emptying, forgave sins, He did so just because His Incarnation made Him one with humanity. And the people ' glorified God who had given such authority unto *men.*' Our Lord only exemplified the privilege that belongs to all men. We can, and must, say 'We forgive them that trespass against us' only because we can, as human beings, say 'Our Father.' But the plural pronouns, as elsewhere in the Lord's Prayer, refer to all mankind. So that when we put together the two clauses 'Forgive *us*—as *we* forgive' we can make them mean 'Let there be, in earth as it is in heaven, universal forgiveness.'

But here we are confronted with a difficulty. Christ said 'Forgive your enemies.' That command, in all its immensity and simplicity, was new in human thought. But what did He mean ? and how much ? Forgive your enemies ; forgive the Germans and the other enemies who have desolated more than a continent with blood and fire. What does He mean ? and how much ? I believe that this problem, which is troubling so many hearts finds its solution in the Lord's Prayer. The thought ' in earth as it is in Heaven ' permeates the whole Prayer. Everything that we pray for in human life is to be a counterpart of something that is found in the life of God, because He is our Father, and we as His children are to reproduce Him. And what have we learnt about our Father's forgiveness ? ' Thou forgavest them, O God, and punishedst their own inventions.' Anyone who believes that the war is the result of human sin, in other words that it is God's instrument of punishment, can with perfect sincerity be ready to forgive Germany, and at the same time pray that she may be defeated for her spiritual good, for the hallowing of His Name, the coming of His Kingdom, the doing of His Will. It is difficult to measure the extent of the wrong notions which have arisen from the weak sentimentality which imagines that God's forgiveness means the letting off from punishment. And human forgiveness must be similar in nature to, must indeed be one with, His forgiveness. It must be of the same character. Man can forgive only because God does. It is another case of 'in earth as it is in heaven.' Our readiness to receive the Germans back into unity with mankind, like God's readiness to receive them back into unity with Himself, is such that it will take effect when they are sorry. That is how God treats us: '*if* we confess our sins He is faithful and just to forgive us our sins.' It takes two to make a quarrel, and it takes two to make it up again. Forgiveness is the readiness to receive back into unity. It acts 'automatically' when the other side is penitent. But as long as they are not sorry, they reject the offer and postpone the unity.

Now if this is the true nature of forgiveness, based upon the oneness of mankind, we ought not to feel it difficult to forgive them that trespass against us. If we feel it difficult, it is because we are making it a personal matter, which, as I have said, is the extremity of futile arrogance. And if we feel that we are doing a very kind and good and pious action in forgiving, we have made the same mistake. If my brother sin against me seven times in the day—seventy times seven—every time he repents I must, as the representative of humanity, perform the completely impersonal act of receiving him back into unity with humanity. To hesitate to do it, or to be pleased with myself for having done it, is to forget that it is simply the impersonal duty of a representative.

And this makes another point clear. 'If ye forgive not men your trespasses, neither will your Father forgive your trespasses.' To refuse to forgive one who has wronged you, and has repented, is to do all that in you lies to shut him out from the oneness with humanity which he seeks. But the effect of that is that while God brings him back by forgiveness, you have shut yourself out. Our Lord's words do not imply a sort of tit-for-tat retribution: 'If you don't forgive you shan't be forgiven.' They express something that lies in the very nature of things—in the principle of representation, which penetrates all human life.

But we can go further. Though we sometimes do a wrong to a definite person, and that person is the representative of mankind who ought to forgive, we far more often do wrong of other kinds. All the sins, negligences, and ignorances of our spiritual life — are these committed against God, or against man? The Psalmist could say 'Against Thee only have I sinned,' because he rightly felt that a wrong done to an individual as such was as nothing compared with the wrong done to God. But what of all sin, including our most secret faults, such as pride, for example, or insincerity, or wandering thoughts in prayer? Of course they are sins against God, and we need His forgiveness to reinstate us in our oneness with Him, our office of representing Him. But they are also, none the less, sins against the whole of mankind. Because of the oneness of all mankind every sin, however private, and however little it may seem to affect anyone else, drags down not only the individual sinner but the whole body of humanity. An instrument in an orchestra that is played too loud, or out of tune, or out of time, is not simply spoiling its own performance, it is spoiling the perfection of the performance of the entire orchestra. Since we are representatives of God and of humanity, our sin is alienating us from oneness with God, and also injuring humanity—injuring it as truly by a secret, sinful thought as if we had done a definite injury to a definite person. And therefore mankind—the whole of humanity—must forgive us—reinstate us in unity, in our office of representing the whole body.

But how can the whole of humanity forgive us for a sin which is not committed against an individual member of it? There is one group of persons in the world that exists for the express purpose, among other purposes, of bringing sinners back into unity with God and man, namely the Catholic Church, the Body of Christ who is the true Mediator. The Catholic Church in Christ Jesus is, so to speak, officially the priest of humanity. But again, how can the whole Church express its forgiveness? One group of persons within the Church exists for the express purpose, among other purposes, of bringing back into unity with God and man any sinner who is sorry, and says so. They are those who are officially ' chosen from among men ' to act as priests. Humanity in Christ is God's sacrament, His outward means of expressing Himself. And the Christian priest represents the Church which represents humanity; He is God's sacramental means, in Christ, for the purpose of forgiveness.

But we can close this chapter by returning once again to the words of the Prayer. 'Forgive *us our* trespasses.' That can mean Forgive all mankind, living or departed. Do we put that meaning into the sentence constantly? And since forgiveness cannot take effect till the sinner is penitent, we are really praying that all human beings, living or departed, may be sorry for their sins; that men and women and children may repent before they die; but if not, that God in His mercy will grant them further opportunities of repentance, forgiveness, cleansing, and restoration. All whom the world calls hopeless, the hardened criminals who have spent most of their life in prison, the thieves and extortioners, the forgers and liars and cheats, the cruel and cowardly bullies, the neglecters of their children, the drunkards, the murderers, the men who ruin women, and the women who ruin men, *and* the great mass of so-called respectable people who go comfortably and selfishly through life caring not one scrap what is happening to the souls around them—they are all made, together with us, to be representatives of humanity, and made in the image of God. We therefore join ourselves with them in penitence, and on their behalf as well as our own we say ' Our Father, forgive us our trespasses.'

VI. TEMPTATION AND EVIL.

'LEAD us not into temptation.' Here is another instance in which the order of the sentences is important. Think of a person who has been living in sin ; and the good Shepherd has mercifully gone after him until He has found him, and has cast down his opposition and hardness and wilfulness, and given him a broken and contrite heart, and received Him back into union with Him by divine forgiveness. We know well that when that happens it is not the end and completion of his spiritual life but only a fresh beginning. He must constantly say ' Lead us not into temptation ' *after* ' Forgive us our trespasses ' has been answered. And the same is true of the religiously minded person, the worker for God. He is burdened from time to time with the knowledge that he has made a great many mistakes in his work, that he has not filled it with prayer as he intended to do, that his spiritual life has been getting dull, and

TEMPTATION AND EVIL

blunted, and low. And then with a contrite confession he has flung himself into God; and his heart is made so fresh and clean and peaceful that he feels for the moment as though there could never be any trouble again. But he knows well that *after* he has been forgiven his trespasses is the moment that he must at once begin again to pray ' Lead us not into temptation.'

From the order of the sentences we turn to study the words themselves. What is the difference, as regards temptation, between human beings and the lower animals? Picture a flat plain, and a mountain rising from it. The lower animals are placed on the flat; man is placed on the slope above. The force of gravitation is always pulling downwards. But the animals on the flat don't feel it; for them it is, so to speak, no pull at all, because they cannot be drawn lower than they are, and they have no wish to rise higher. But man, on the slope, must either go up or down; that is he must either overcome, or yield to, the pull of gravitation. This pull is like the natural instincts of our animal nature, in other words it represents temptation in its elemental, fundamental force. It never ceases; we are so made that we are never without it for one second of our waking life ; it lies in the very nature of things. But while we possess animal bodies our true self is nevertheless made in the image of God ; and that image has been revealed, and renewed in mankind, in Jesus Christ. And therefore we have the power of climbing upward, of overcoming step by step the downward drag.

But if that is so, we can say with certainty that it is not wrong to be tempted. God Himself has given us our animal bodies ; He has caused this force of gravitation to be always at work, pulling at us ; He has placed us on the slope expressly in order that we may overcome and climb upwards. And we may gain further comfort from the fact that our Lord was tempted—really tempted—all His life long.

But what, then, did He mean by the words, ' Lead us not into temptation ' ? Look again at the climber on the slope. The work of overcoming the downward pull of gravitation is hard enough without any other difficulties ; but it becomes very much harder if he meet with rain, wind, snow, fogs, glaciers, falling rocks, and all the other dangers of a high mountain. That, I think, was what our Lord meant. He was not thinking of temptation in its elemental, fundamental nature, but of things which add to the natural difficulty of growing in holiness. And into these we are to pray that we may not be led.

Now although we have had a good deal of experience of temptation, we are not always able to express our thoughts about it clearly. We pray, for instance, ' Grant Thy people grace to withstand the temptations of the world, the flesh, and the devil.' We read in the Epistle of S. James (i. 13), ' Let no man say when he is tempted, I am tempted of God ; for God cannot be tempted with evil, neither tempteth He any man. But every man is tempted when he is drawn out by his own lust and enticed.' But in the very same chapter (*v.* 2) we meet with the words, ' Count it all joy when ye fall into divers temptations ' ; and (*v.* 12), ' Blessed is the man that endureth temptation.' We are told that God did tempt Abraham. And when our Lord said to S. Philip ' Give ye them to eat,' the evangelist adds ' This He said tempting him, for He Himself knew what He would do.' Are temptations good or bad? It seems at first sight as though the word ' temptation ' must have two quite distinct meanings. God does not, of course, tempt men in order to make them sin ; that is clearly what is meant in the first passage quoted from S. James. On the other hand God tested, or tried, Abraham, and our

Lord tested, or tried, S. Philip, not for his harm but for his good. We might be inclined, therefore, to say that temptation is bad, and trial or testing is good. But a little thought will shew that that explanation doesn't work. You say that so-and-so is a dreadfully trying person to live with, and you find it very hard not to lose your temper frequently ; which is it, a temptation or a trial ? Or you have for some time been feeling unwell, tired out, or in frequent pain, or worried, anxious, overworked. You have had, you say, a dreadfully trying time, and it felt almost impossible to keep your spiritual life at the level that you wanted to keep it ; which was it, a temptation or a trial ?

And another distinction that we are rather apt to make. We mostly use the word ' trial ' of things that feel nasty—troubles of some sort, whether of mind or body ; but ' temptation ' may be something that is all too pleasant and enticing. It is a temptation, for instance, to some people to stay in bed too late, so that they don't leave time to say their prayers properly. But that is not usually called a ' trial.' On the other hand they would probably call it a trial if it was a headache or toothache, or an exacting invalid, that made prayer difficult.

But all these distinctions are quite wrong.

'Temptation' and 'trial' are translations of exactly the same Greek word. All trials are temptations, and all temptations are trials. It simply depends on which way you look at them. You are on the slope of the mountain amid endless difficulties. The gravitation of your lower nature is always pulling one way, and God with the chords of love is drawing you the other way. If you slip downwards you have yielded to temptation, and you have sinned. If you overcome in the power of God and climb upwards, you have stood the trial, the divine test for the purifying and strengthening and growth of your soul.

With these thoughts before us, the true meaning for the Christian of 'Lead us not into temptation' becomes clearer. Whenever we say it we must add in thought, 'If it is Thy will.' Instead of 'Give us this day our daily bread,' we might say 'Lead us not this day into hunger.' But if hunger is good for us, God will show His love best by not giving us daily bread. In the same way, when God sees that some trial, some temptation, is good for us, He will show His love best by leading us into it; and when that happens we can 'count it all joy,' as S. James says. Think of the temptation that troubles you most grievously, and most often.

You have the Lord's own warrant for saying 'Our Father, lead me not into it.' But you have His warrant also for adding 'Nevertheless not as I will, but as Thou wilt.' You can, as S. Paul did, pray over and over again that the thorn of the flesh, or the thorn—shall we say—in the mind, may depart from you. But you must be ready for Him to say, if necessary, 'My grace is sufficient for thee.'

At the same time, which of us can guess from how many thousands of temptations or trials He has kept us in answer to our prayers? He knows us so well—our differences, our circumstances, our upbringing, our heredity, our temperament, our powers; and He will never suffer us to be tempted, or tried, above that we are able.

And so when we come to the last words we find their meaning plain and simple. 'Lead us not into temptation, but—*whatever happens*—deliver us from evil,' or in other words, 'deliver us from sin.' Evil means sin and nothing but sin. Pain is not evil, sorrow is not evil, no sort of trouble or trial is evil, no temptation is evil. Nothing in heaven or earth or under the earth is evil except sin.

Lastly, as in other petitions in the Prayer, we must lay stress on the plural pronoun. ' Deliver *us* from evil ' means Deliver us all—all men, and women, and children—from sin. We must strive to make our prayer, with a growing reality, as wide as the human race. Our Father which art in heaven, deliver us all from sin. Thou hast placed us all above the rest of the animals ; Thou hast, in Thy love, given to all men, and women, and children, the glory of being able to rise voluntarily to Thee, the glory of climbing, the glory of overcoming. Draw us all with the chords of love, that we may go from glory unto glory, from height to height, from strength to strength, till unto the God of gods appeareth every one of us in Zion.

VII. THE KINGDOM.

'FOR Thine is the kingdom, the power, **and the glory, for ever and ever. Amen.**' Our Lord did not teach these words to His disciples; they were added by the Christian Church some time afterwards for the purpose of public worship. But they are deeply suggestive and worth studying.

Notice first the way in which the sentence was attached to the Prayer. ' Deliver us from evil, *for* Thine is the kingdom.' That is to say, the kingdom, the rule, the sovereignty, does not belong to evil but to Thee. ' Evil,' as we have already reminded ourselves, means sin and nothing but sin. And when we say ' Thine is the kingdom,' we mean ' Thine ideally—Thine by right,' although at present sin does its utmost to usurp Thy throne. Which has it been lately in our hearts ? Two kings cannot sit upon one throne. No one can be slave to two masters. Know ye not that to whom ye yield yourselves slaves to obey, his slaves ye are whom ye obey ? We know this as a theory, but we so often act as

THE KINGDOM

though we did not think it was really true. We find ourselves slipping into the lazy feeling that on the whole things are going on all right in our hearts. We don't say it of course, but this is the sort of thing that we are apt to feel: I acknowledge God as King certainly, and in a general way I always want to please Him; I do my duty, my religious, and social, and—at the present moment especially—my charitable duties; on the whole I think I do them rather well. But of course I am human; I can't expect to be perfect; and if I am sometimes a little selfish, or envious, or snappy, or irritable; if I do sometimes find myself criticising other people and running them down, and liking to hear them run down; if I do sometimes forget God's presence and love for hours, possibly days, together; if my thoughts do wander rather frequently at prayer and worship; if they do occasionally slip into what is actually bad; if I do sometimes lose my temper, and grumble, and fret, and feel horrid; in other words, if I do very often sin—it is only human after all, and God is very good and lenient, and has promised to forgive my sins; and anyhow I am a Christian and miles better than a great many other people. Those are the times that we need the reminder that two kings cannot sit upon one throne. At the moment that any one of these things has been true of us, or anything else that our conscience tells us of, we have thrust God from His throne and put sin there instead. God says, ' Thou shalt have none other gods but Me.' But at these moments—and they really occur very often !—Self cries, Thine is not the kingdom ; I am king, and there is none else.

And God cannot forgive us, that is His readiness to forgive cannot take effect, until we repent ; until we confess with sorrow that we have dethroned Him until we cry ' Oh, remember not our old sins—our old, old sins that come back so often—but have mercy upon us.' Take, O Lord, Thy power and reign once more in my heart, ' for Thine is the kingdom.'

But we can next take a wider outlook. The struggle against evil in my heart is a minute reflexion of the struggle between good and evil in the whole history of the whole world. And here we have a thought of restful and abiding comfort. Deliver us—deliver the whole world—from evil, for Thine is the kingdom. The Lord is King, be the people never so impatient ; He sitteth between the cherubim be the earth never so unquiet. The waves of the sea are mighty and rage horribly, but yet the Lord who dwelleth on high is mightier. The Lord sitteth above the

THE KINGDOM

waterflood, above the clash of nations in arms, and the Lord remaineth a King for ever.

Now when we speak of God's Kingship we are using human language, as we are obliged to do whenever we try to say anything about Him. And an earthly king is a very poor type. But we can think of some characteristics of ideal kingship. Let us dwell upon the thought of the perfect King.

Consider first the function of an earthly king. He combines, theoretically, in his own person, the functions of every individual subject. Every subject is his representative, but the office and duty of every one is found, ideally, in him for the rule and welfare of the state. And through these millions of representatives he possesses, ideally, the knowledge needful for all this. And God also has His countless millions of representatives; but He knows, in microcopic detail, more than any one of them. Grasp of detail is one of the surest marks of a great mind. Caesar, Napoleon, and all the most famous leaders of men possessed it. No detail was too small to receive their full attention, because their minds were great enough to see the part that the detail would play in working out a large design. If we carry this up to an infinite degree we come to God's knowledge of detail.

Every detail is to Him of infinite—literally infinite—importance, because it plays an essential part in His eternal plan. This cannot be pressed too strongly. When He gives us duties to do, it is utterly wrong to say that in His eyes this duty is more important, and that duty is less important. Both are part of His plan, and therefore both are of infinite importance; and both are given equally His full divine attention.

We know this of course; we have been told it very often. But very often it has been a mere theory, and not a bit real to us. If we could only grasp it as a solid truth it would be such a help. The 'smallest' duties, as we call them, are not small to God, because to Him the infinitesimal is infinite. Something comes before us of which we say, 'Well, it's got to be done,' and we are tempted to add, 'but it's an awful nuisance; it takes up so much valuable time when I might be doing something more important.' At moments like that, moments of drudgery, moments of irritation at household or family vexations, moments when we should like something more exhilarating than mere routine, moments in fact when we hanker after something that is *not* our duty, the whole thing would be put right if we could lift up our hearts and say, 'Thine is the kingdom.' Thou dost govern all things in heaven and earth. This bit of dull routine, this irritation, this nuisance—Thou knowest it in detail; it is part of Thine eternal plan; Thy full divine attention is given to it; to Thee it is of literally infinite importance. 'Thy kingdom come,' a little nearer to fulfilment by my doing this duty well; 'Thy will be done' by this bit of drudgery. The great thing is that because He is the perfect King, He knows and cares.

And it is only in this spirit that we can face the war. Every precious life apparently thrown away; every limb shattered apparently to no purpose; every unseen act of heroism that no-one in this life will ever speak of or remember; every hidden heartache at home for the dear one who has suffered or died; because God is the perfect King, He knows and cares about every one, individually, in detail, because every one of them has formed part of His eternal plan. Thine is the kingdom, for ever and ever. Amen.

But when we think of the war in this way it helps to give us, what we all need so much, a wider and vaster conception of God. Among the many things that the war is doing it is helping to lift comfortable Christians at home out of their little self-centred circles of thought—lift them to a hill top, so that they can get a larger view of the world lying around them. As Isaiah put it, ' They behold a land of far distances.' That was the great strength of the Hebrew prophets. They got up so high, so near to God, that they could stand, as they said, like watchmen on a tower, and could see further than anyone else. God's Kingship is so grand. And the nearer we get to His point of view, the more we can see of His plan, and realise how the far distances stretch away into infinity.

For instance, many minds find an acute problem in the sufferings of animals, the undeserved sufferings of innocent animals, tortured and devoured by other animals and by man ; the whole creation groaning and travailing in pain together. We must, of course, do all that we can to alleviate the sufferings of animals as of men ; but still there remains the gigantic mass of pain. And we dare not face it unless we can take a vast outlook and say, ' Thine is the kingdom.' ' God is the King of all the earth,' therefore ' sing ye praises with understanding,' in spite of the huge volume of suffering which ye cannot understand. Since God is the perfect King He knows and cares about every detail, every pain of every sparrow that falls. He is working out His eternal plan, and in His infinite love He allows pain to be one of His chiefest instruments. We don't know why. But we are not God. He knows why, because He is King.

Or take another difficulty. Here we are in the year 1916 after Christ, and the world is not Christian yet ; large tracts of it have never been been preached to, not to speak of converted. Europe is not Christian yet, as the war proves clearly enough. England, we like to think, is the best country in Europe ; but how much of it does God think of as Christian ? Thousands profess no religion, and many thousands more profess to be Christian and are not. England, as a whole, still needs to be converted. And we cry, Lord how long ? We had hoped that there was at least a basis of Christian morality, resting on which the nations of the world were, by civilised methods, building up permanent brotherhood and peace. But it has all been shattered at a blow. And some are asking, Has Christ failed ? Is Christianity soon to be a matter of past history ? And some go further and say, Where is now thy God ? And all of us who long and pray for the fulfilment of the world's redemption through our Lord Jesus Christ are inclined sometimes to complain in despair that it is so terribly slow in coming.

But when we feel pessimistic we must brace

ourselves with the thought, Thine *is* the kingdom, however long it may be in coming. And after all there are helps in the matter. Geology and astronomy alone ought to teach us that 1,900 years are the merest nothing. If a being from another planet could watch a small stream carving its way through a hill of solid rock, or coral insects building an island that is to be many square miles in extent, with its roots as deep as the sea, he would probably say that it was a terribly slow process. But God the King has His plans, and centuries are nothing to Him. Christianity is still in its early infancy. And what right have we to say that spiritual processes must be quicker than physical? The most elementary faith in the governance of the world by God ought to make every Christian an optimist, not with the cheap optimism which says, with its eyes shut, that everything is going on as well as possible, but with the unshakeable certainty that throughout the immeasurable lapse of centuries the kingdom is the Lord's, and that He is carrying out His vast, slow plans.

In the meantime we who love Him a little must look to ourselves. I am a detail in His plan. And however infinitesimal I appear when I look at the huge sweep of the ages, nevertheless the perfect King devotes His whole attention to me, a detail, because to Him the infinitesimal is infinite. Am I doing my best for Him ? Do I pray with my lips two or three times a day, ' Thy kingdom come,' and then delay its coming by my want of love, want of prayer, want of humility, want of self-restraint, want of real eagerness to advance His kingdom, want of real surrender to his will ? And so we come back, as we must always come back, to the thought of penitence. Thine is the kingdom, and I dethrone Thee every day. ' Oh, hearken Thou unto the voice of my calling, my King and my God, for unto Thee do I make my prayer. Forgive me, O Lord, forgive me ; and come and reign in my heart more completely than I have ever let Thee reign before.

VIII. THE POWER.

WE have been thinking of the perfect King. His governance of all things in heaven and earth, His entire knowledge of every detail, His concentrated attention given to every detail, and His age-long plan to which every detail contributes. And the more we contemplate the breadth, and length, and depth, and height of His kingship, the nearer we approach to an insight into the immeasurable vastness of His Power. 'All Thy works praise Thee, O Lord, and Thy saints give thanks unto Thee. They shew the glory of Thy kingdom and talk of Thy power; that Thy power, Thy glory, and the mightiness of Thy kingdom might be known unto men. Thy kingdom is an everlasting kingdom, and Thy dominion endureth throughout all ages.' After saying 'Thine is the kingdom,' it seems almost superfluous to add 'the power.'

And yet the word 'power' is full of valuable meaning. The Greek word denotes ability to do things. But a whole world of thought is opened up when we remember that God is able

THE POWER 73

not to do things. Power purposely restrained can be the highest exercise of power. Let us think, then, of the power of God as shown in His Self-limitation. An earthly king does not possess the power of governing every detail in his kingdom with direct, personal knowledge and activity ; he is compelled to manage his realm by means of thousands of representatives. But God, who knows every infinitesimal detail infinitely, does He need helpers ? Why should divine power need assistance ? And yet we know that every member of His kingdom, every man, woman, and child in His realm, is made to be His agent and helper in the working out of His plan. But that can be only because He deliberately limits Himself, to give us a share in the management. Think of that for a moment. It is something so wonderful ! God wants things done ; there are unnumbered millions of things to be done for the working out of His plan. Why doesn't He do them Himself? Why these long, long ages of delay ? It is because He has willed to display His power by not doing them immediately Himself. He wants to give us the privilege of doing them.

And when we don't do them, we postpone His purposes and delay His plan. But still He never rushes in impatiently, to take the matter out of our hands. The patience of God is an unceasing exhibition of His power. We fail in our work, we fail in our prayers, we fail in our love to Him, we fail, therefore, in the perfecting of our souls, and on that account we fail in our influence over others. But all these things in which we fail are the work that He wants done for the advancement of His kingdom. Of His own deliberate will begat He us in order to be His helpers ; and we mostly hinder. When we walk down the street we pass through a constant stream of people who are made to be His helpers, but are mostly hindering. We go to some other town by train, and find more streams of people who are mostly hindering. And if we travelled for weeks and months, we should find all over the planet hundreds, and thousands, and millions of human beings who are all mostly hindering. Can we wonder that God's spiritual processes are slow ? But He *will* not hurry or be impatient ; He will not force men, or take away their free will. He shows His divine power by exercising it over Himself, limiting Himself by making use of human agents for the working out of His plan. The Lord is King, but He deliberately shares His kingship with us ; it may be called a ' limited Monarchy '—limited by Himself.

But out of this arises naturally the thought that if we are given the power of kings to share with Him, the power of will, the power of working out voluntarily His divine plan, we also in our turn must seek to exercise that power in the highest possible way, that is by deliberate self-limitation. Self-assertion is not the highest exhibition of power. It is because Nietsche's philosophy declares that it is, that it stands at the opposite pole from the religion of Christ. God deliberately preserves to us our free will ; we must respond by deliberately preserving for Him the submission of our will to His. We must limit Self as He limits Himself. This power must be exhibited ' in earth as it is in heaven.'

We can long for nothing greater than to be more ready and able for real self-sacrifice, self-discipline, self-forgetfulness, selflessness. We have a picture of it before our eyes every time we open the daily paper. The war means suffering, horror, maddening misery, tragedy reeking with blood and torture known only to those who have seen and felt it. And yet there are the young men from all the five continents who were mostly plain civilians, with all their life before them, life with its untold possibilities of honour and ambition, interest and happiness, some of them recently married, just beginning to surround themselves with the delights of their own new home, or just thrilled with the deep joy of their own new son or daughter. Volumes could not exhaust all that is contained in the strong, healthy life of a young man. And yet millions of them, without a shadow of fuss or bragging, and without a fret or murmur, knowing perfectly well what they were doing, with their eyes wide open to all the loss and terror and agony, and, hardest of all, knowing perfectly well what it would mean to those left behind, deliberately laid down all that life offers, at the mere call of duty, feeling that no decent man could do less.

And the higher the motive that leads a man to this act of self-emptying, the nearer it brings him to an imitation of the self-emptying of Christ. Upon the Cross He gathered up, and offered to His Father, all the selflessness found in any human life in the history of the world.

Now when we contemplate all this, it touches us hard, it thrills us to the core, we know and feel that there is no power to equal the power of selflessness. Gaze long enough, and closely enough, at the spectacle of supreme self-sacrifice, and it almost hurts with the intensity of its beauty. But—the next moment—some little detail, some little duty or drudgery or bother of daily life crops up, some little opportunity of self-crucifixion, and the dazzling vision fades, our soul drops to its old low level, as we thought a moment before that it never could drop again, and we find that in our own case self-sacrifice is a horribly dry and dreary thing; it seems to have no halo round it, no one perhaps will ever hear of it, much less speak about it, and we discover that the wood of the Cross is very hard, and the nails are torture. We learn, in other words, that selflessness needs more power than anything else in the world.

Let us, at this point, be very exact and unsparing with ourselves. We know that 'self-sacrifice' and 'love' are negative and positive expressions for the same thing. We can test the extent to which we have attained to the power of selflessness by examining ourselves with the help of S. Paul's inspired description of love.

Love suffereth long. It bears uncomplainingly troubles, worries, bothers, routine, drudgery, disappointments. It meets them all with the unmoved patience of selflessness. Love suffereth long, *and is kind.* That is to say, not only is it never unkind, but it searches eagerly, restlessly, joyfully, for every possible chance of being kind ; and especially at home, because it knows that if it fails to exercise the great power of selflessness at home it won't be worth much anywhere else. *Love envieth not*. It envieth not other people's money, their houses, or motors, or books, or opportunities of travel, or any other outward and visible possession ; it envieth not their natural gifts and talents, their intellectual ability, their physical ability, their artistic ability ; it envieth not their popularity or personal charm, or social position ; it envieth nothing and nobody, because to be crucified with Christ means to share in His Self-emptying. *Love vaunteth not itself*. It never boasts, never pushes itself forward in conversation, never sacrifices strict truth in order to say something smart ; it never wants to create a sensation, or force itself into notice, or make itself talked about ; it never bores other people with its own doings or interests, its own ailments or worries, while it is always ready to listen to theirs. *Love is not puffed up*. It is never even secretly proud of its own doings and successes and virtues ; it never thanks God that it is not as other people are, and is never self-satisfied ; it never resents a rebuke or criticism ; it never fails in any of the thousand little ways in which it has an opportunity of practising a deep and instinctive humility. *Love doth not behave itself unseemly.* It avoids like poison the faintest trace of undue freedom in voice or manner or action or thought. *Love seeketh not her own.* It doesn't stickle for its rights, or stand on its dignity; it doesn't think that any action for other people, however small or bothersome, is a waste of time. It doesn't 'seek its own' because selflessness, by its very definition, has already given up all that is its own. *Love is not easily provoked.* No irritation—think of it!—absolutely no irritation can easily provoke it, because real selflessness is buried deep in the peace of God which passeth all understanding. And Love *thinketh no evil.* It never criticises other people without real and urgent necessity; it always says something good about them if it possibly can, and, for the rest, keeps its lips impenetrably closed; it never enjoys hearing other people criticised and run down; and even in its secret thoughts it tries hard not to dwell on, or remember, other people's failings and foibles, knowing what its own temptations are.

But it seems so hopeless! The ideal is so high. S. Paul is surely mocking us when he says ' Let this mind be in you which was also in

Christ Jesus.' No, we can fall back on the words that we are studying, ' Thine is the kingdom, and the *power*.' If God Himself shews His power by Self-limitation, He can also shew it by giving it to us. ' Not by might, nor by power—that is Not by human might or human power—but by My Spirit, saith the Lord of Hosts.' If God the Father exercises kingship over our lives, God the Holy Spirit exercises power in our hearts. There is only one sure and certain method of arriving at power over Self, and that is to live in the atmosphere of power, to live in the Spirit. The climber in the Alps has to struggle against, and overcome, the steady persistent, downward drag of gravitation. And the struggle, the exercise of free will, the voluntary determination to get to the top, are his own. He would indignantly refuse the offer of a funicular railway to carry him to the summit. Most of the value of the climb consists in the very struggle. But we know how it is that he has become an experienced mountaineer—how it is, for example, that the Swiss guides become so extraordinarily expert. It is because they are incessantly in the high air, doing exploits. In our spiritual struggle we must live a high mountain life, always breathing the Spirit of God, if we are to become experts.

To drop the metaphor, and come to the plain, unvarnished truth; if we are to become increasingly successful in overcoming Self, we must pray more, and pray better. We must not be content with the average level of Christianity which confines prayer to set times, and rather brief times at that. To get the power of the Spirit we must live in it, and walk in it. When we say to God the Holy Spirit, ' Thine is the power,' it means that, like a shellfish in the ocean, we are compassed about with infinite power, and we have only to open wide the doors of our soul to drink it in.

IX. THE GLORY.

THE kingdom, or sovereignty, of God works inwardly by power. We thought of it in God's own Being, the power of Self-limitation; and then we thought of it as the power of the Holy Spirit in man, enabling him in his turn to exercise the supreme power of selflessness. But after the kingdom and the power we add ' and the glory.' This word needs careful study, because it is used in the Bible with various shades of meaning. But the principal meaning which includes all the varieties is this: ' glory ' is power as it is seen, visible, intelligible, manifested, recognised. To put it shortly, ' glory ' is power become apparent. When we speak of glorifying God, or bringing glory to God, we mean acknowledging, or leading other people to acknowledge, a manifestation of His power. ' They shew the glory of Thy kingdom, and talk of Thy power; that Thy power, Thy glory, and the mightiness of Thy kingdom might be known unto men.'

Let us follow the same lines as in the last chapter by thinking first of God's own Being. His power of Self-limitation becomes apparent in its effects. It becomes apparent in the created universe. That anything in heaven or earth or under the earth should have what we call a finite existence of its own involves an unceasing limitation of the Infinite and Absolute. When, therefore, we say, ' Thine is the glory,' let us not forget the glory of God in Nature. Natural science cannot rightly be divorced from religion ; it is a continual wondering investigation of the Self-limiting power of God. But natural science by itself is only an accurate observation of events and sequences. We want to get nearer to the glory than that. It is a great spiritual help, which can be gained more easily by some temperaments than by others, to immerse the senses in natural beauty of any kind, provided the beauty is recognised as the glory of God, the outward expression of the inward power of Spirit at work. ' The sunset touch, the chorus from Euripides ' can both make the Christian chant his *Gloria*.

To see God's glory in Nature is the first step. But we must not be content till we see it without the aid of the senses. What God can be to the human soul varies with the ability of each soul to feel after Him and find Him. Those who did so more profoundly than most men generally tried to describe their experiences under the form of intense light. The power of the Spirit became so apparent to them that they seemed to themselves to be visualising the glory. Glory does not mean light ; but throughout the Bible, in almost every attempt to describe God's glory, a shining light is used as the verbal expression of it. Now this ability to come into vivid contact with God's glory is a gift, as music or poetry is a gift. It is not everyone who can be a S. Theresa, as it is not everyone who can be a Beethoven or a Browning. But it is possessed in some degree by everyone, and remains latent until it is cultivated. Sheer contemplation of God as He is in Himself is entirely neglected by the great mass of Christians. To detach the soul by concentration, and a steady purpose of the will, from all intellectual thought about God, or about anything, and in a deep, still silence of the whole being to desire Him, to strive and reach and grasp at Him, to drink in His love, and at the same time to throw the whole Self upon Him in the love that He wants —that is the way in which the great saints gain their wonderfully vivid perception of His glory. And even the distant approach to it which is

THE GLORY

possible for every Christian lifts the soul away from earthly things, and helps it to live in the Spirit.

But when we have thought of God as He is, God who dwelleth in the light that no man can approach unto, the full sight of whose glory is the beatific vision, which we cannot see till we know as we are known, we are led to another truth. We said that God limits Himself to give us a share in the power of His Spirit. But that means also that He gives us a share in His glory.

Think how He did it. He came with His spiritual power into mankind in the Person of Jesus Christ. ' We beheld His glory, the glory as of an Only-Begotten of the Father.' And Jesus Christ could say, ' The glory which Thou hast given Me I have given them.' During His earthly life the glory was veiled ; but by His Resurrection He was fully and finally glorified. In the risen Christ the power of the Spirit was fully and finally displayed, and made available for all mankind. In S. James ii. 1, according to what is probably the best reading of the Greek, the expression actually occurs ' our Lord Jesus Christ the Glory.' But we have already noticed that in the Bible ' glory ' is constantly thought of as a shining light. Hence to the non-Christian the call comes ' Awake thou that sleepest and arise from the dead, and Christ shall give thee light '—Christ shall give thee a share in His glory when thou lettest His Spirit begin to make His power apparent within thee. And to the Christian the call is, ' Arise, shine, for thy light is come, and the glory of the Lord is risen upon thee.' ' Ye were sometime darkness, but now are ye light in the Lord. Walk as children of light.'

This truth, when rightly understood, gives an extraordinary exhilaration to the Christian life. It is not a mere weary struggle against sin; it is not a mere effort to satisfy God enough to get to heaven; above all, it is not a mere self-satisfied piety. The risen Christ in all His glory is in us, and we are to be luminous with His light. ' The glory of the Lord doth shine in it, and the lamp thereof is the Lamb.' That is true not only of the perfected city of God, the triumphant Church of the redeemed; it can be true now of the heart of every Christian, and becomes more and more true as he passes ' from glory unto glory.'

But that brings us back to the old, sad fact. If the light of the glory of Christ is shining within me, why am I not luminous? Why is my soul so dull, and opaque, and dark, and black? Because Self prevents me from shining. Thine,

O Christ, is the glory within me, but mine is the thick veil that hides its radiance. The Christian life, therefore, is the gradual stripping off of the veil, that the light may shine ; it is the killing of Self, that the Christ in me, the power of His Spirit in me, may become more and more apparent.

But, lastly, let us ask, Why must I try to be luminous with the divine glory ? It is not that I may gain the satisfaction of developing a beautiful character. It is not that I may escape the anger of God. It is not that I may finally reach the joys of heaven. There are many wrong motives that might influence me. But there is only one motive that really exhilarates life. We must say to God, ' Thine is the glory,' and therefore, *because it is Thine own*, Thou dost long to see it and enjoy it. Thou hast limited Thyself by Thine Incarnation. Thou hast limited Thyself to allow me to do Thy work voluntarily. But Thy desire is that I should respond to that limitation, and satisfy Thee by exhibiting to Thee Thine own glory with an ever increasing brightness, until the day comes when Self is killed, and I am nothing but glory for Thy sake, no particle of my being shall remain that is not dominated by Thy Spirit, **there shall be nothing in me but Christ.** The satisfaction of God is the satisfaction of His Love, which yearns to see Himself in me, unclouded and undimmed. For that I exist, and with any lower object it were better that I had not been born.

Thine is the kingdom, O Father, Lord God Almighty; and I will kill Self that Thou mayest reign within me.

Thine is the power, O Holy Spirit ; and I will kill Self by that power within me.

Thine is the glory, O Jesus Christ the Son, the manifestation, of God ; and I will kill Self that Thou alone mayest shine within me.

And all this in order to satisfy the Love of the Three Persons in One God, the Holy and Eternal Trinity.

www.ingramcontent.com/pod-product-compliance
Lightning Source LLC
Chambersburg PA
CBHW071726040426
42446CB00011B/2240